R Level 3.4

R Points .5

153928

SMOKE JUMPER

BY NICK GORDON

BELLWETHER MEDIA · MINNEAPOLIS, MN

Are you ready to take it to the extreme?
Torque books thrust you into the action-packed world
of sports, vehicles, mystery, and adventure. These books
may include dirt, smoke, fire, and dangerous stunts.
WARNING: read at your own risk.

Library of Congress Cataloging-in-Publication Data

Gordon, Nick.
 Smoke jumper / by Nick Gordon.
    p. cm. -- (Torque: dangerous jobs)
 Includes index.
 Summary: "Engaging images accompany information about smoke jumpers. The combination of high-interest subject matter and light text is intended for students in grades 3 through 7"--Provided by publisher.
 ISBN 978-1-60014-781-4 (hardcover : alk. paper)
 1. Smokejumpers--Juvenile literature. 2. Smokejumping--Juvenile literature. 3. Wildfire fighters--Juvenile literature. I. Title.
 SD421.23.G67 2013
 628.9'2--dc23

                          2012003338

This edition first published in 2013 by Bellwether Media, Inc.

Printed in the United States of America, North Mankato, MN.

A special thanks to Mike McMillan for contributing images.

TABLE OF CONTENTS

CHAPTER 1

WILDFIRE!

An airplane flies over a forest fire. Giant clouds of smoke hang above the land. No fire trucks can reach this fire. The only people who can fight the flames are smoke jumpers. They check their gear and strap on their parachutes. Then they leap out of the plane.

Special Delivery

Chain saws and other heavy equipment are dropped from airplanes separately. They float down with their own parachutes.

The smoke jumpers sail through the smoke-filled air. They land only a few hundred feet from the blaze. They cut down trees and brush in the fire's path. The fire grows closer as the smoke jumpers soak this **firebreak** with water. They finish just in time. The fire reaches the firebreak and slowly dies out. The smoke jumpers have done it!

CHAPTER 2

SMOKE JUMPERS

Smoke jumpers are highly trained firefighters. Their job is to **contain** wildfires. Smoke jumpers go where normal firefighters cannot. They often parachute near forest fires and are on their own for days.

Gone With the Wind

Spotters throw long rolls of paper out of planes to learn wind direction and strength. However, winds can change mid-jump.

Sew Talented

Smoke jumpers learn to sew during their training. They are responsible for repairing their own parachutes.

Smoke jumpers go through intense training. They must be in great physical shape. Machines lift smoke jumpers into the air and then drop them. This training teaches them how to survive crash landings.

Smoke jumpers also learn how to fight wildfires. One main task is to remove **fuel** from a fire's path. Smoke jumpers cut down trees and brush. They also dig **trenches**. This creates a firebreak. They may soak an area with water or a **fire retardant**. Sometimes smoke jumpers light small, controlled **backfires**. These fires use up the fuel that a wildfire needs to spread.

Splashdown

Smoke jumpers learn to gather their parachutes after a water landing. They must stay calm and work quickly if they become tangled in the parachute lines.

CHAPTER 3

DANGER!

Smoke jumpers face constant danger. Jumping out of a plane is risky. It is even more life-threatening when the ground below is on fire. Thick smoke makes it hard to see. Strong winds can push a smoke jumper off course. Missing the target landing area can be deadly.

Wildfires are **unpredictable** and often spread faster than expected. Smoke jumpers risk severe burns and **smoke inhalation**. They also risk broken bones. Smoke jumpers often have to climb trees to cut them down. No one can rescue them if something goes wrong.

Smoke jumpers need special gear to stay safe. They wear padded **Kevlar** jumpsuits. They also wear strong **harnesses**, protective helmets, and fireproof gloves. Smoke jumpers use a **let-down rope** to **rappel** to the ground if they land in a tree.

In the Field

Smoke jumpers can spend days or weeks fighting a fire. They carry enough food and water for about two days. Aircraft must bring them more supplies.

Smoke jumpers work in some of the most dangerous environments on Earth. They confront fires that most people would run away from. Every jump into a flaming forest could be their last.

Tragedy on the Job

On July 6, 1994, three smoke jumpers and eleven firefighters died in a huge wildfire in Colorado. The fire spread up to 18 miles (29 kilometers) per hour. Flames grew to a height of 300 feet (91 meters). The smoke jumpers could not escape.

Glossary

backfires—small, controlled fires set by smoke jumpers to rob wildfires of the fuel they need to spread

contain—to stop from spreading

fire retardant—a chemical that stops a fire from burning

firebreak—an area where trees and brush have been cleared away; firebreaks rob a wildfire of the fuel it needs to spread.

fuel—any material that helps a fire grow and spread

harnesses—straps that connect smoke jumpers to parachutes

Kevlar—a brand of very strong fiber, often used in bulletproof vests and other gear that must absorb powerful impacts; some Kevlar is fire-resistant.

let-down rope—a rope a smoke jumper uses to get to the ground if stuck in a tree

rappel—to descend while attached to a rope

smoke inhalation—injury caused by breathing in smoke

trenches—long, deep ditches dug into the ground

unpredictable—having behavior that is hard or impossible to guess

To Learn More

AT THE LIBRARY

Holden, Henry M. *Fire-Fighting Aircraft and Smoke Jumpers*. Berkeley Heights, N.J.: Enslow Publishers, 2002.

Reeves, Diane Lindsey. *Scary Jobs*. New York, N.Y.: Ferguson, 2009.

Trammel, Howard K. *Wildfires*. New York, N.Y.: Children's Press, 2009.

ON THE WEB

Learning more about smoke jumpers is as easy as 1, 2, 3.

1. Go to www.factsurfer.com.

2. Enter "smoke jumpers" into the search box.

3. Click the "Surf" button and you will see a list of related Web sites.

With factsurfer.com, finding more information is just a click away.

Index